PLANET IN PER

TSUNAMI SURGES

Cath Senker

First published in paperback in 2015 by Wayland
Copyright © Wayland 2015

Wayland, an imprint of Hachette Children's Group
Part of Hodder & Stoughton
Carmelite House, 50 Victoria Embankment
London EC4Y 0DZ

Editor: Elizabeth Brent
Designer: Ray Bryant
Cover design by Rocket Design (East Anglia) Ltd.

Dewey number: 363.3'492-dc23

ISBN   978 0 7502 8909 2
Library eBook ISBN   978 0 7502 8537 7

Printed in China

10 9 8 7 6 5 4 3 2 1

Picture acknowledgements: All images courtesy of Shutterstock.com except: Cover image © AFLO / MAINICHI NEWSPAPER/epa/Corbis; p4 © REX/KeystoneUSA-ZUMA; p5 © REX/Miyako City Officer; p6 © Getty Images/Dorling Kindersley; p8 © MIKE NELSON/epa/Corbis; p10 © Anton Croos; p12 © ALTAF HUSSAIN/Reuters/Corbis; p13 © iStock/ EdStock; p15 © A.S. Zain / Shutterstock.com (t); p16 © REX/KPA/Zuma; p17 © U.S. Geological Survey; p18 © Getty Images; p19 © IVAN ALVARADO/Reuters/Corbis; p21 (t) © BradCalkins; (b) © AFP/Getty Images; p22 © REX/Quirky China News; p24 © KYODO/Reuters/Corbis; p25 (l) © KYODO/Reuters/Corbis; (r) © iStock/1001Nights; p26 © AFP/ Getty Images; p27 © Jesper Rautell Balle

Text acknowledgements: p11 Eyewitness: Sunday Observer, Sri Lanka, 16 January 2005; p13 Case study: Kimberley Sevcik, World Volunteer Web, 5 May 2006; p15 Eyewitness: 'They Lived Through It: Tsunami Survivor Stories', Catholic Relief Services, 2013; p19 Case study: 'Chilean city reborn after 2010 quake and tsunami', 26 February 2013, Global Times; p23 Eyewitness: Japan tsunami eyewitness stories #3 by Kasper Nybo, 18 July 2011; p25 Case study: 'JKTS: A Japanese medical aid worker's diary', 15 October 2011; p27 Expert view: 'NEES tsunami expert says improved research tools helped predict impact of this week's Japan earthquake', Phys.org, 11 December 2012; p29 Expert view: 'Coastal Protection', MIT Mission 2009 Tsunami team 2.

An Hachette UK company
www.hachette.co.uk
www.hachettechildrens.co.uk

Contents

What are tsunamis?

Have you ever thrown a rock into a pond? It shifts the water and creates waves. These waves move outwards, carrying energy.

ON A FAR BIGGER SCALE

When there's a major undersea earthquake or volcanic eruption, the seafloor shakes violently, displacing a huge amount of water. It creates gigantic, powerful waves in the ocean that race away at up to 800 km (500 miles) an hour — that's as fast as a jet plane!

When a wave nears the shore, it slows down. But as the seabed becomes shallower, the water is forced to swell upwards. The wave can rise to a fearful height of up to 30 metres (about 100 feet) — as high as a ten-storey building. Beware: a tsunami is coming.

Tsunamis and tides

You might hear a tsunami being called a 'tidal wave'. This is wrong! Tsunamis have nothing to do with the tides. The pull of gravity from the Sun, planets and the Moon causes tides, whereas tsunamis are caused by a major disturbance in the water. However, the tide level affects the height of the tsunami when it reaches the shore — if it's high tide, the wave may be higher.

SWEEPING ASHORE

As the first giant wave approaches the shore, the coastal water is often sucked back dramatically. Then the wave sweeps ashore with enormous force, pulling people, wildlife, boats, large rocks and other heavy debris in its path. It can uproot trees, wash away cars and destroy buildings. The tsunami travels inland up to several kilometres until it has used up all of its energy. As the wave flows back to the sea, it wreaks further devastation, and this may not be the only wave. A series of tsunami surges can batter a coastline over several hours.

If people spot a tsunami, they run as fast as they can to escape.

What causes tsunamis?

Tsunamis occur in coastal areas where earthquakes, volcanoes and landslides are common. Most tsunamis are caused by earthquakes. The majority are low-magnitude events that do not cause great damage. Destructive large-magnitude tsunamis are less frequent.

To understand tsunamis, you need to know about the Earth's plates. The Earth's crust is broken into separate plates, which are slowly shifting towards and away from each other.

When they meet, they slip and slide against each other, moving up, down or sideways. This area of stress is called a fault.

The shifting plates release energy in seismic waves, which can cause huge cracks in the ground – an earthquake. If this happens underwater, the movement can cause a tsunami.

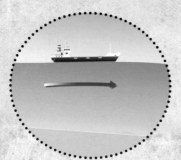

The plates are moving slowly.

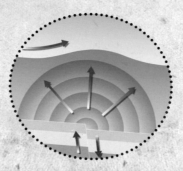

The plates move at the fault.

The shifting ground causes a tsunami.

VOLCANOES

Volcanoes can cause tsunamis too. A volcano on land may erupt, sending ash and debris into the water. This displaces a vast quantity of water, triggering a tsunami. Alternatively, the eruption of an underwater volcano can displace the surrounding water. Landslides are another cause – rocks falling into the sea can create a tsunami.

GLOBAL WARMING

Scientists worldwide are discussing whether global warming is leading to more tsunamis. Glaciers put a lot of pressure on the Earth, but they are melting. When they melt, the pressure is reduced. Experts believe that the changing pressure on the Earth's crust can cause earthquakes, tsunamis and volcanoes.

FACT BOX

Worst tsunamis in history

1. **Indian Ocean,**
   26 December 2004
   Waves up to 15 m (49 feet) high
   At least 234,000 people died

2. **North Pacific Coast, Japan,**
   11 March 2011
   Waves more than 10 m (33 feet) high
   More than 18,000 people died

3. **Lisbon, Portugal,**
   1 November 1755
   Waves up to 30 m (98 feet) high
   60,000 people died

In *Tsunami Surges*, we'll look at three dramatic and devastating tsunamis and find out what happened, along with the impact of each tsunami, and how the stricken communities recovered. We'll also investigate technologies that can help us to cope with this ferocious hazard to our planet.

It is 7.59 a.m. on Boxing Day, 2004.

Just off the coast of Aceh in Sumatra, Indonesia, a massive undersea earthquake occurs, with a magnitude of 9.1 on the Richter scale. This earthquake lasts a full five minutes – longer than any ever recorded. The epicentre is very shallow – just 20 km (12 miles) deep.

The earthquake triggers a series of huge tsunami surges that spread across the Indian Ocean over the next seven hours and affect thirteen countries. With no early warning, Indonesia, India, Malaysia, the Maldives, Sri Lanka and Thailand all suffer major damage. It is the biggest tsunami ever known, and one of the most destructive natural disasters in history.

WHAT CAUSED THE TSUNAMI?

The earthquake happened when the Indo-Australian plate was subducted (forced down) under the Eurasian plate, which lifted the seafloor along a fault line over 1,000 km (over 600 miles) long. This displaced billions of tonnes of seawater above, triggering the tsunami.

A ruined house in Aceh after the tsunami.

THE TSUNAMI STRIKES

In open ocean, the tsunami measured under 1 m (3 feet) high, and it travelled at a speedy 800 km (500 miles) an hour. When it hit Sumatra, the waves were travelling at 40 kph (25 mph) and were about 24 m (80 feet) high. Witnesses heard the noise of the approaching tsunami, like the roar of a jet plane. In several places, the ocean pulled back alarmingly, exposing the seafloor and stranding fish and boats. The wave rushed over the land, reaching 4 km (2.5 miles) inland. Many people managed to escape but others could not run away fast enough. The wave then surged back out as rapidly as it had arrived. Large numbers of people who had survived the incoming tsunami were swept out to sea as it retreated. After striking Asia, the tsunami travelled nearly 5,000 km (3,000 miles) to east Africa and still had enough force to kill people and destroy buildings there.

Size of waves:
15 m (49 feet)

Speed of waves:
800 kph (500 mph)

Number of people killed:
at least 234,000

Number of people homeless:
About 1.8 million

Cost to the economy:
US $9,930 million

Deaths and destruction

Because of the extent of the devastation, it is hard to know the exact death toll but it is estimated that, overall, more than 225,000 people in the affected countries lost their lives, as well as 9,000 foreign tourists.

Indonesia, Sri Lanka, India and Thailand suffered the worst. The death toll was highest in Indonesia, the first-hit country, particularly in Aceh. More than 200,000 people were killed in Indonesia alone.

Some people died because they were curious to see the exposed seafloor, or went to gather fish and were drowned as the tsunami thundered in. Interestingly, animals seemed to know disaster was on the way; they fled for high ground before the tsunami arrived. Many people had no chance to escape as entire villages and towns were destroyed by the tsunami. Along the low-lying coast of Aceh, many buildings made of wood were simply swept away. Several fishing villages in Tamil Nadu, India, were completely wiped out.

HAZARDS FOR SURVIVORS

Many people were injured, or became homeless – 500,000 in Sumatra alone – and families were separated while trying to escape. The floodwaters contaminated the water supply, leading to diseases such as cholera, and survivors endured a lack of food and medical treatment. Wildlife suffered too; animals were stranded, fish supplies were devastated and farmland was ruined.

Eyewitness

The man who saved his village

Victor Desosa, headman of Galbokka village in Badulla, Sri Lanka, had been a sailor. He remembered how the water had shaken in Valparaiso, Chile in 1982, just before a massive earthquake:

'On December 26 [2004], I was down by the ocean, talking to a friend, and I saw that the water was shaking. . . . I did not know exactly what was happening, but the feelings I had in Chile were back and I knew we had to get out of our village. I began to hoot and shout to people to run inland, to run up on the hills.'

As they got to high ground, a 6-m (20-foot) wave smashed into Galbokka. In other similarly affected villages, up to a half of residents perished. Because of Desosa's quick thinking, just one person died in Galbokka.

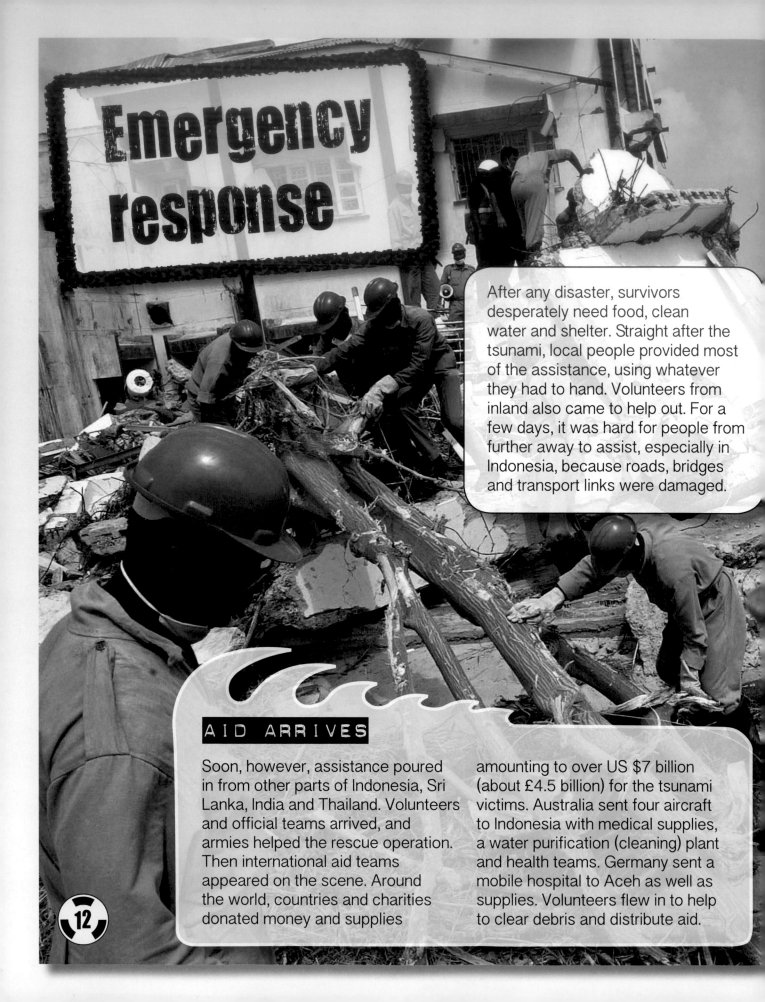

Emergency response

After any disaster, survivors desperately need food, clean water and shelter. Straight after the tsunami, local people provided most of the assistance, using whatever they had to hand. Volunteers from inland also came to help out. For a few days, it was hard for people from further away to assist, especially in Indonesia, because roads, bridges and transport links were damaged.

AID ARRIVES

Soon, however, assistance poured in from other parts of Indonesia, Sri Lanka, India and Thailand. Volunteers and official teams arrived, and armies helped the rescue operation. Then international aid teams appeared on the scene. Around the world, countries and charities donated money and supplies amounting to over US $7 billion (about £4.5 billion) for the tsunami victims. Australia sent four aircraft to Indonesia with medical supplies, a water purification (cleaning) plant and health teams. Germany sent a mobile hospital to Aceh as well as supplies. Volunteers flew in to help to clear debris and distribute aid.

*The US hospital ship USNS **Mercy** on her way to the Indian Ocean to help victims of the tsunami.*

A huge clean-up operation began. Mass graves were dug to bury the dead quickly and try to prevent disease from spreading. Experts worked to restore the water and power supplies. The Red Cross and other charities provided clean water and sanitation to people who had been displaced by the tsunami.

Case study

A volunteer helps to rebuild a house in Sri Lanka.

Aid worker helps rebuild homes

Kimberley Sevcik travelled from the USA to Sri Lanka ten weeks after the tsunami, to join a team constructing new homes in Bataduwa village, Galle. The volunteers worked under the instruction of Sri Lankan builders, using traditional methods. No power tools or cement mixers were available - they used pickaxes and shovels. Kimberley learnt how to mix concrete, fit boulders together to build a wall and make support columns. The tough, physical work under the ferocious sun was exhausting, but one day, Kimberley met the family whose house they were building. They were living under a piece of tarpaulin, on a thin mattress on the ground. Kimberley knew then that her efforts were worthwhile.

Lost livelihoods

As well as losing loved ones, many people lost their homes and way of life. Fishing boats were washed away, and cafes and beach shacks destroyed. Salt and floodwater ruined growing crops and damaged land. It took up to 18 months for the soil to recover. In Sumatra, 400,000 people lost their livelihoods in fishing, tourism and agriculture. Overall, one million people were left with no means to make a living.

RECONSTRUCTING COMMUNITIES

Once the debris had been cleared, governments and aid agencies provided assistance for local people to build new homes and boats for fishermen. Charities such as Oxfam helped to build new wells and water systems. However, reconstruction took a long time. In Indonesia, people spent months in temporary camps before being rehoused.

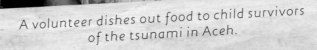

A volunteer dishes out food to child survivors of the tsunami in Aceh.

Marwani rebuilds her life

Marwani lived in Suak Bidok in Aceh, Indonesia, metres from the sea. She said the wave approached with a noise 'like a train'. Marwani grabbed her two youngest children, aged five and thirteen months. 'The children held onto my shoulders, but they were torn free when I was knocked over,' says Marwani, 'I was carried inland [more than a mile].' She, her husband and oldest two children survived. They sheltered in a tent provided by Catholic Relief Services. After a year, they received materials to build a semi-permanent home with wooden walls and a metal roof. The village has since been rebuilt with better houses than before, with electricity and plumbing. Marwani has had another child, although she never stops thinking of those she lost. 'Day by day, month by month, we are trying to get past what happened,' she says.

A refugee camp for victims of the tsunami in Aceh.

BETTER PREPARATIONS

Governments and aid agencies also invested in preparing people better for future tsunamis. They put up signposts to show evacuation routes and taught people drills so they would know what to do if disaster struck again. Improved tsunami warning systems were also adopted (see page 26).

พื้นที่เสี่ยงภัยคลื่นยักษ์
TSUNAMI HAZARD ZONE

IN CASE OF EARTHQUAKE, GO
TO HIGH GROUND OR INLAND

เมื่อเกิดแผ่นดินไหว ให้หนีห่าง
จากชายหาดและขึ้นที่สูงโดยเร็ว

IT'S 27 FEBRUARY 2010.

A huge earthquake measuring 8.8 on the Richter scale strikes off the coast of south-central Chile, caused by a rupture along the fault separating the South American plate from the Nazca plate. The stress of the enormous, crashing plates shatters rocks along the boundary between them.

The epicentre is about 325 km (200 miles) south-west of Santiago, the capital. The quake is so strong that people can feel it in Buenos Aires, Argentina and São Paolo, Brazil. The earthquake's focus is about 35 km (22 miles) beneath the Pacific Ocean's surface. A portion of the seabed is forced upwards, displacing the water above and causing a tsunami. The Chilean town of Constitución is pummelled by waves up to 15 m (49 feet) high, and a 2.4-m (8-foot) wave strikes the port of Talcahuano.

NO WARNING

Although Chile has a tsunami warning system, it failed. The government did not issue a warning immediately after the quake, which could have allowed many in the path of the giant wave to evacuate to higher ground. The president, Michelle Bachelet, claimed the failure was due to a breakdown in communications in the region and incorrect data from the navy about the earthquake's location. She told a magazine, 'The first information about a tsunami that I received was people calling from [the Chilean islands of] Juan Fernandez saying they had been hit.'

Owing to the lack of warning, around 150 people died in the tsunami. In the coastal areas struck by the wave, there was massive destruction of boats and buildings, and the port of Talcahuano was damaged. Dichato was one of the worst-affected places; around 80 per cent of the town was destroyed. Fishing boats weighing at least 10 tonnes were lifted by the waves and dumped around 3 km (2 miles) inland.

Size of waves:
15 m (49 feet)

Speed of waves:
800 kph (500 mph)

Number of people killed:
521 in total; 150 in tsunami

Number of people homeless:
2 million (earthquake and tsunami)

Cost to the economy:
US $30 billion

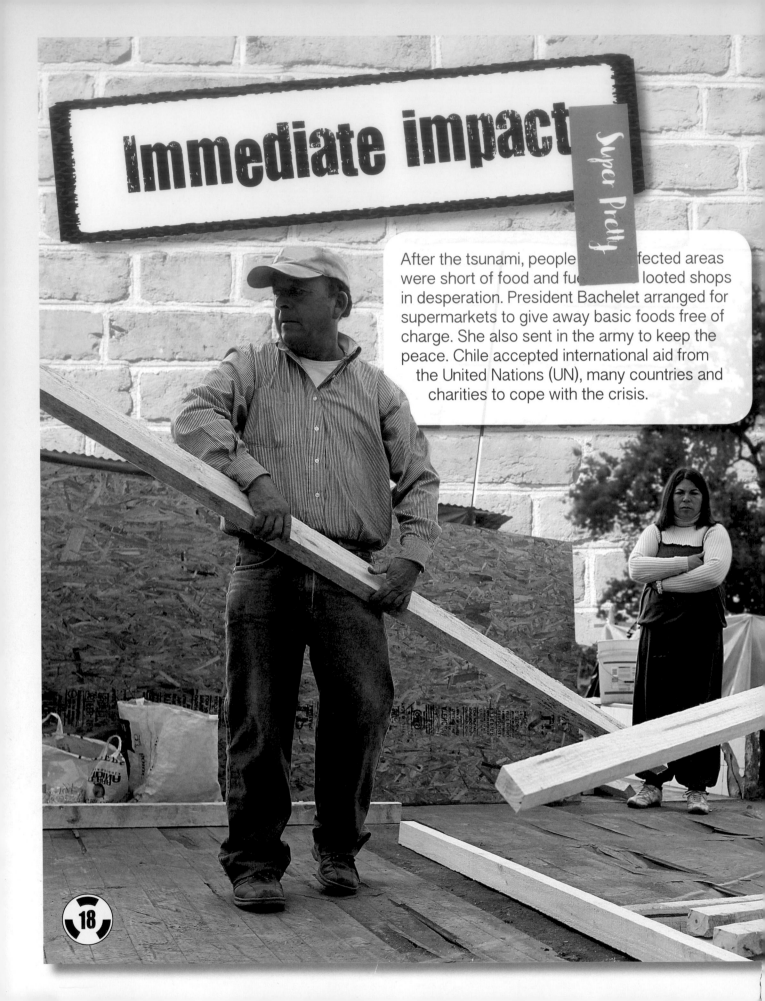

Immediate impact

After the tsunami, people [in the af]fected areas were short of food and fue[l, and] looted shops in desperation. President Bachelet arranged for supermarkets to give away basic foods free of charge. She also sent in the army to keep the peace. Chile accepted international aid from the United Nations (UN), many countries and charities to cope with the crisis.

REBUILDING

Some people displaced by the tsunami lost their homes, while people in the fishing and tourism industries lost their livelihoods. For example, Dichato had previously attracted around 10,000 people per year to enjoy water sports and the beaches. Its shellfish industry was ruined because the water became contaminated and filled with debris. Three years later, around 75 per cent of those made homeless had new homes. Many streets and buildings had been reconstructed, but other areas had yet to be rebuilt. A similar situation existed in other damaged towns.

Some residents of Constitución protested in 2011 because they felt the government had not rebuilt homes quickly enough.

ADAPTING FOR THE FUTURE

To ensure people are better prepared in future, people in the affected areas are learning emergency planning and evacuation routes, and being trained to help tourists if disaster strikes again. Those responsible for the failure to warn people about the tsunami have been punished. In May 2012, eight officials were charged with negligence (failure to do their job properly). It can only be hoped that next time the tsunami warnings will save lives as intended.

Case study

Crisis in Constitución

Constitución was battered by waves that destroyed about 222,000 homes, along with hotels, restaurants and other coastal buildings. About 100 people died, mostly on Orrego Island, at the mouth of the Maule River. The government plans to build a buffer-zone park on the island and riverside to avoid deaths and destruction in a future tsunami. It has already invested in new housing and streets to serve as evacuation routes. Survivor Silvia Rojas Opazco says, 'I lost everything in the tsunami and it was just like starting over again. I have been living here for two months, in my new apartment, with my husband and son. We are much better off than before because the new apartment is bigger, and this building has solar heaters.'

The story of the 2011 tsunami begins with a huge earthquake of magnitude 9 off the north-eastern coast of Japan's main island, Honshu.

The epicentre is about 130 km (80 miles) east of Sendai, Migayi Prefecture, and the focus is 30 km (19 miles) below the Pacific Ocean floor. During the earthquake, the Pacific plate suddenly thrusts horizontally and vertically, displacing the water above and triggering a series of tsunami waves.

COASTS BATTERED

Hundreds of aftershocks follow the initial earthquake, leading to devastation on land. But it is the tsunami that proves most destructive. Sendai, Iwate, Fukushima and other low-lying coastal areas are hit by giant waves up to 10 m (33 feet) high. In places, the water rushes several kilometres inland — up to 10 km (6 miles) near Sendai.

20

The tsunami crashes over many sea walls 5–12 m (16–39 feet) high; they do little to reduce the impact of the waves. As the floodwaters retreat, they carry a huge quantity of debris – many victims are caught up in the flow and perish. Large areas of land are completely submerged by seawater. This is one of the deadliest disasters in Japan's history.

WHAT WENT WRONG?

Japan, a country with a known risk of tsunamis, has sophisticated early warning systems. Special detectors in the Pacific Ocean estimate when the waves will arrive. When they detect an earthquake, emergency sirens go off and sensors close the floodgates. People hear the sirens and use the escape routes. However, the epicentre of the earthquake was so close to the shore that there was little time to inform the public of the approaching disaster and give them time to evacuate.

Size of waves:
10 m (33 feet)

Speed of waves:
800 kph (500 mph)

Number of people killed:
at least 18,500

Number of people homeless:
450,000

Cost to the economy:
US $360 billion

Devastation

Some towns were almost completely destroyed. An estimated 95 per cent of the coastal resort of Minamisanriku was flattened – just some taller buildings remained. In some places, including Minamisanriku, half of the population went missing. Although many were found, between 18,500 and 20,000 people perished. The vast majority drowned in the tsunami waves; more than 50 per cent of the victims were over 65. The survivors were in a dire situation: 4.4 million people were left without electricity and 1.5 million people without clean drinking water. About 114,000 homes were destroyed.

NUCLEAR MELTDOWN

To add to the crisis, Japan was struck by a major nuclear accident when tsunami water damaged the cooling systems for the six nuclear reactors at the Fukushima plant. As the water spilled over the sea walls, it caused hydrogen (gas) explosions and fires. Huge amounts of radiation leaked into the surrounding area, and the authorities had to evacuate everyone within a 20-km (12.5-mile) radius. The radioactive vapour contaminated water and food supplies around Fukushima. In July, the evacuation zone increased. People within a 29-km (18-mile) radius were advised to leave or remain indoors to protect their health.

Narrow Escape

Sachie was at home with her one-year-old baby Kouka when the tsunami hit. She recalled, 'Kouka was having a nap when the earthquake occurred. I grabbed my baby straight away and ran outside. The earth was shaking ... and the tsunami was approaching us. As I saw the size of the tsunami, I realized I wouldn't survive if I stayed inside. So I carried Kouka... and ran up the hill as fast as I could. When I reached the top of the hill, I saw my house was washed away by tsunami.

It was snowing that day and very cold. I stayed the night outside with 13 other neighbours... When the dawn came, fire department officers came to rescue us. We were frightened that [the] tsunami might come again, so we moved on quickly… We walked all the way until we could see the rescue bus, and I think it was about 4 o'clock that afternoon when I finally arrived [at the] shelter.'

Rescue operation

After the tsunami, the Japanese Self-Defence Force and many rescue workers rushed to the worst-affected areas; 116 countries offered money, food, medicine, doctors and search teams. The Red Cross and the Red Crescent sprang into action. The catastrophic damage to transport and communications systems made it hard for rescue workers to reach the victims. Terrible weather conditions in the first few days, with mud and debris covering the ground, hampered their efforts further. Nevertheless, many people were rescued from the rubble. Several hundred thousand people who had lost their homes found their way to shelters.

ECONOMIC EFFECTS

Fukushima and Miyagi were responsible for 40 per cent of Japan's economic output. After the disaster, most manufacturing stopped but within a few weeks, buildings and transport systems were repaired. By early 2012, industrial production had returned to its pre-tsunami level.

NUCLEAR CRISIS CONTINUES

The nuclear accident proved a bigger problem. For several months, radiation levels in the evacuation zone remained high. Some people returned to the five towns just outside of the 20-km (12.5-mile) evacuation zone, but others stayed away owing to fears about radiation. Radiation leaks continued to occur at the site where contaminated reactor cooler water was stored, including a major leak in August 2013.

THE RECONSTRUCTION PROCESS

The Japanese government provided a large budget for reconstruction in 2011, and the following year set up an agency to coordinate reconstruction. In 2013, 300,000 people were still living in prefabricated housing units or other temporary housing in Sendai. Reconstruction is certainly going to be a long job.

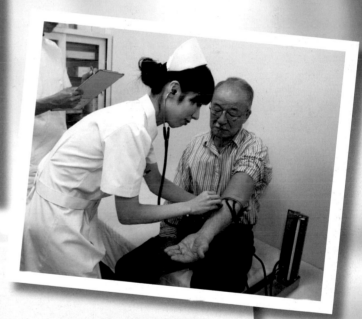

Case study

Emotional support

A Japanese nurse from Tokyo went to Minamisanriku six months after the tsunami to perform health checks for people in temporary housing units. It seemed that the general environment had improved, although work was required to make sure that babies and elderly people could live comfortably through the winter. However, she found that survivors needed emotional support. She met a woman who had lost all her family and workmates on that fateful day. The woman stared at her mobile and said, 'Most of the people in my address book are dead.' The nurse found that offering her friendship was the most useful thing she could do.

Prediction and protection

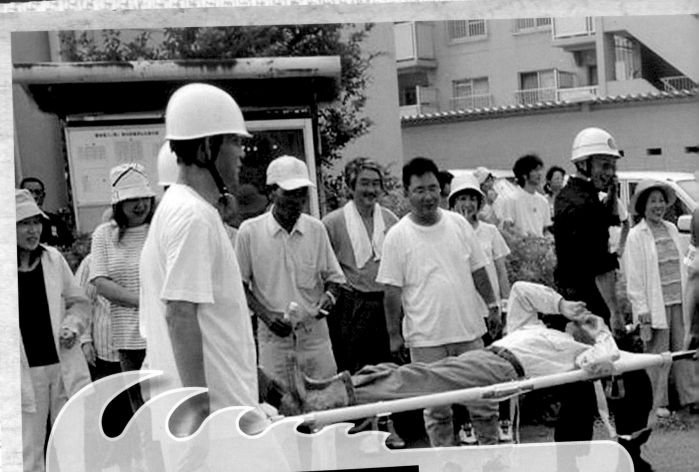

HOW TECHNOLOGY CAN HELP

Technology can help scientists to forecast tsunamis accurately so people can be warned to escape to higher ground. In 2005, the United Nations (UN) set up the Indian Ocean tsunami warning system, at a cost of around US $20 million. Also, the National Oceanic and Atmospheric Administration (NOAA) has developed a tsunamograph.

A recorder sits on the bottom of the ocean and measures changes in water pressure caused by alterations in the water level. It sends signals to a buoy, which transmits measurements of the wave heights to a satellite. Scientists look at the data to work out the strength of the tsunami and whether they need to warn people to evacuate.

26

Prediction success

The prediction of earthquakes and tsunamis has improved since the 2011 disaster. In December 2012, leading tsunami researcher Solomon Yin stated that better research tools helped the accurate prediction of the tsunami risks of an earthquake near Japan. Just eight minutes after an earthquake of magnitude 7.3, an information bulletin was sent out declaring that 'no destructive widespread tsunami threat exists'. Yin commented, 'The system worked. This is a real success story in terms of more accurately predicting in real time what the impact might be.'

Residents take part in a tsunami drill in Gobo, Wakayama Province, in 2005. It's important to know how to act if there's a tsunami warning.

LOW-TECH SOLUTIONS

Despite improved prediction techniques, a tsunami may arrive hot on the heels of an earthquake and there is little time to warn people. So it's vital to teach people in high-risk areas to spot the warning signs and act quickly. Low-tech solutions are crucial, such as clear signposts on beaches. Also, people may not have time to reach high places, or the buildings nearby might not be tall enough to protect them. Evacuation platforms are tall structures that people can climb in an emergency. In Japan, many have been built since the 2004 Indian Ocean tsunami.

COMPUTER MODELLING

Experts also use computer modelling to work out the effects of tsunamis on different coastlines. With this information, local people can work out escape routes and determine the height of land they need to reach to be safe.

Natural defences

Around the world, growing numbers of people are living near coasts. How can they be protected from tsunamis? In Japan, the government is building tall, wide sea walls to defend coastal communities from tsunamis. However, environmentalists are concerned that these are damaging seaside ecosystems. They block the movement of wildlife between the land and the sea, and destroy habitats such as sand dunes.

A longer-term solution might be for people to move away from the coast and resettle further inland, leaving nature intact along the shore. Then both habitats and people would be protected. Yet, it is not practical for people relying on fishing and coastal tourism to live away from the coast.

A dead coral reef, killed by polluted seas and global warming.

RESTORE NATURAL PROTECTION

Another option is to look to nature. Human activity has reduced the natural protection of the coast from tsunamis. Many countries have harmed coral reefs and cut down coastal mangrove trees, which are natural ways of blocking the force of a tsunami. Coral reefs are made of living organisms stuck to rock. As a tsunami wave moves over the top of the reef, its energy is reduced, weakening the wave before it smashes into the coast. Mangrove forests absorb and disperse (spread out) tsunami surges. Working to restore coral reefs and mangrove forests, combined with sophisticated prediction technology, could protect people from the ravages of future tsunamis.

Expert view

Trees - tsunami busters

The students on MIT Mission 2009 researched how to limit tsunami damage: 'One of the most effective methods of protection from a tsunami is trees. Some villages in India, for example, had minimal casualties in the 2004 tsunami because they had planted trees along the coastline. The village of Naluvedapathy [in Tamil Nadu] . . . was protected by about a kilometre [-thick] of trees and suffered no direct damage from the tsunami. Even though this would be too many trees for many areas of the coastline, a moderate thickness of trees, especially those with deep roots and dense coverage, can protect effectively against tsunamis. Mangroves, it appears, are especially good at protecting areas from tsunamis, so a beach with mangroves on the shore and rows of trees behind it would be well-suited to withstand a tsunami.'

Glossary

buffer zone   In coastal places at risk from tsunamis, an area where people are not allowed to live.

buoy   An object that floats on the sea, usually to mark where it is safe for boats to go. A buoy can also be used as part of a tsunamograph, to pick up signals from the bottom of the ocean.

casualties   People who are killed or injured in a disaster or war.

cholera   A disease caught from infected water that causes bad diarrhoea and vomiting, and often results in death.

computer modelling   Using a special computer program to model a real-life situation, such as a tsunami hitting the coast.

contaminated   Made dirty because of substances added to it.

debris   In tsunamis, all the things that have been swept up by the waves, such as wood, household goods and rubbish.

displacing   Moving something from its usual place.

environmentalist   A person who is concerned about the natural environment and wants to improve and protect it.

epicentre   The point on the Earth's surface, directly above the focus, where the effects of an earthquake are felt most strongly.

evacuation   Moving people from a place of danger to a safer place.

fault   A break in the Earth's crust where the plates on either side have pushed against each other.

focus   The point within the Earth where an earthquake starts.

forecast   A statement about what will happen in the future, based on information that we have now.

glacier   A large mass of ice, formed by snow on mountains, that moves very slowly down a valley.

global warming   The increase in temperature of the Earth's atmosphere that is caused by the increase of particular gases, especially carbon dioxide.

gravity   The force that attracts objects in space towards each other, and that on Earth pulls them towards the centre of the planet, so that things fall to the ground when they are dropped.

looted   To steal things from shops or buildings, usually after a riot or disaster.

magnitude   A measurement of the power of an earthquake.

mangrove   A tropical tree that grows in mud or at the edge of rivers and has roots that are above ground.

nuclear reactor   A large structure used for the controlled production of nuclear energy.

plate   One of the very large pieces of rock that form the Earth's crust.

prediction   A statement that says what you think will happen.

prefabricated housing   Houses made in sections that can be put together where they are needed.

radiation   Powerful and very dangerous rays that are sent out when there is an accident at a nuclear power station.

reconstruction   Rebuilding something that has been damaged or destroyed.

Richter scale   A system for measuring how strong an earthquake is.

rupture   When something breaks or bursts.

sanitation   The equipment and systems that keep places clean, especially by removing human waste.

satellite   An electronic device that is sent into space and moves around the Earth or another planet. It is used for communicating, for example by radio or television, and for providing information.

seismic waves   Waves caused by earthquakes that release energy.

subducted   When one of the Earth's plates is forced under another one.

United Nations   An association of most of the world's countries that aims to improve economic and social conditions and to solve political problems in the world in a peaceful way.

vapour   A mass of very small drops of liquid in the air.

Find out more

Books

Non-fiction

Deadly Waves: Tsunamis by Mary Dodson-Wade (Enslow Publishers, Inc., 2013)

Earth in Action: Tsunamis by Jennifer Swanson (Core Library, 2013)

Floods and Tsunamis by Doreen Gonzales (PowerKids Press, 2012)

Natural Disasters: Tsunamis by Richard Spilsbury and Louise Spilsbury (Wayland, 2012)

Tsunamis and Floods by Gary Jeffrey (Franklin Watts, 2010)

Fiction

Child With No Name by Valentine Williams (Kindle Edition, Amazon Media)

I Survived the Japanese Tsunami, 2011 by Lauren Tarshis (Scholastic, 2013)

Running Wild by Michael Morpurgo (HarperCollins Children's Books, 2010)

Tsunami! by Kimiko Kajikawa (Philomel Books, 2009)

Websites

The Deadliest Tsunami in History?
http://news.nationalgeographic.co.uk/news/2004/12/1227_041226_tsunami.html
About the Indian Ocean tsunami

Earthquake in Japan
www.scholastic.com/browse/collection.jsp?id=822
Articles about the earthquake and tsunami written by kids for kids.

Indian Ocean tsunami: Interactive guides
www.theguardian.com/tsunami/interactive/0,,1381082,00.html
How the tsunami occurred; how it affected each country; tsunami warning systems.

Tsunami – How a Tsunami Happens
http://academic.evergreen.edu/g/grossmaz/springle/
How earthquakes, volcanoes and landslides cause tsunamis.

Tsunamis – Natural History Museum
www.nhm.ac.uk/nature-online/earth/volcanoes-earthquakes/tsunami
The causes of tsunamis and scientific research about them.

Tsunamis – an Underwater Earthquake hazard
www.coolgeography.co.uk/GCSE/AQA/Restless%20Earth/Tsunamis/Tsunamis.htm
How tsunamis occur and the events of the Indian Ocean tsunami.

Film

Tsunami – The Killer Wave – The Compelling & Moving Story As Seen on the BBC (IMC Vision, 2005), exempt from classification
Personal stories and interviews with people involved in the Indian Ocean tsunami.

Index